Resting in the Secret Place

Resting in the Secret Place

Craig Romkema

Copyright © Craig Romkema

All rights reserved

ISBN-10: 061594731X

ISBN-13:978-0615947310

For my father, who left us all too soon.

Contents

Stream	1
Before	3
Consolation	5
Reconstruction	7
Four Wheels; Two Wheels; Three	10
Addiction	12
Exposure	14
Confession	16
Breathe	18
Sacrifice	20
Borrowed Shelter	22
Spectrum	24
Bizarre, Bizarre	26
.00001	28
In Step	31
Menagerie	33
Morning	35
Seduction	37
One Hour	38
Release	40
Dusk	42
Sleep	44

Attempt	46
Resolution	48
So You Know	50
Reaching	51
Disconnected	53
Risk	55
Lost Friend	57
Midsummer Night	60
Unbound	61
The Fabulous Four Minus Three	63
(In) dependence	65
Emma	67
Rest	69
Passage	71
Flight	73
Unexpected	75
Grace	77
Perchance	79
Eastern Star	80
Just Go	81
Couples	82
Lightkeepers	84
On The Airwaves	86
Longing	87
Coming Down	89
Move	90
Rumination	92

Awakenings	94
ABOUT THE AUTHOR	97

Stream

Why the urge to bring together
thousands of pieces of Favrile glass
into one wisteria lamp--
Clara Driscoll and her Tiffany Girls
spending four days selecting just the right shades,
cutting them into the necessary shapes
and fitting them onto a patterned dome,
then watching the hapless cleaning woman
knocking the table just enough to dislodge
rivers of shimmering glass
into a pool at her feet?

Gatherings and scatterings.

The cosmic Mosaicist of universes
beyond universes
gathers us together for a time,
then disperses us into some other
grand imagining.

Like pebbles on a seashore tossed together by the tides,
then drawn apart into deep waters;

yellow maple leaves blazing in a cerulean sky,
then moldering into damp earth;
rose petals unfurling in the morning dew,
then drifting into the wind;
blackbirds swirling in spirals,
then stretching out into long lines;
vast herds migrating across desert plains,
then dividing into families;
fetal cells coalescing and multiplying,
eventually dying, disintegrating.

Dust to dust,
but in the interim--
oh, what glory!--
gleaming, resplendent
life
flowing swiftly into our
next design.

Before

The house was washed
in sunlight,
laden with dust motes
for my amusement,
a shifting kaleidoscope of thousands,
never still
long enough to be
counted,
although I tried
many times,
willing the hours of my
captive existence
away,
careless weights of time,
drifting free of the normal lifespan
I'd heard I might
endure,
and I thought--
although they didn't know how much
I constantly puzzled,
analyzed, dissected, synthesized,

until I felt full
of my mind's realizations--
thought about every conceivable source
of those random particles,
civilizations, rotting carcasses,
dead skin cells,
remnants of scattered lives.

Why did they float so lightly,
lining nostrils with every inhalation,
present, but virtually
indiscernible?
Would I, like them,
simply exist,
never more than a
curiosity
revealed in certain light,
lost
from life's consciousness
and would the *yes*
of myself
float into oblivion
unknown?

Consolation

Easily the wound closed over my heart
as if never inflicted by gutless words--
"Retard," they sneered at me on the long bus ride home,
but I held these words in my spirit as a sword against
    theirs,
"You are my beloved son, my chosen one, my strong heart,"
words whispered to me in the darkness when all were
    asleep
save myself and the One who stood watch over me,
who still watches over me with such tenderness that
at times it seems more than I can bear.

Half in and half out of this place we call reality,
I stay with that Spirit always whispering near me,
always peace surrounding my belligerence,
nothing on this earth as tempting as His voice,
as His mantle of compassion over me.

Would I want my existence to be otherwise,
immersed in a world where I cannot hear Him clearly?
I cannot breathe without His breath coursing through me.
Sometimes I see others who share that life-breath;

I see Him through their eyes, feel Him in the
places they inhabit,
know that He also inhabits them, that we share
this secret fierce abiding, He in us,
we somehow in His unseen arms.

No, I am lacking much others consider essential.
Even basic manners are stumbling stones for my
worrisome frame,
but I have Him to release truth in the places of deception,
to grant me respite from my body's ridiculousness,
to breathe over my never-forgotten heart.

Reconstruction

Trying to remember what was never instinct
to my interrupted mind,
the instinct of a fist-chewing, floor-crawling,
milk-seeking child;
trying to restore lost learning
into manageable order is a leap into
unknowingness,
a pushing towards goals
undefined.
What happens when thumb and
index finger meet
in delicate union,
lifting, dropping tiny pegs
into minute holes?
Does the brain believe new ventures
are reward for awkward hands
now that two fingers have found
their dance?
Will ligaments and tendons rearrange
their former patterns,
granting litheness, flexibility?

These appendages on my wrists
have done rudimentary duty:
food to mouth,
clothes to body,
lacking finesse,
for only within the cage of a
supporting hand
can they scrawl out unsightly
approximations of letters,
my laughable mark
of authenticity.
Alone, fingers separate,
pencil falls,
eyes wander,
alone, nerves pulse erratically.

Yet, there is this coupling of
virtual strangers,
this grasping of tiny beads
with surprising ease,
this unknown intelligence released
from my memory,
honed through repetition into
common practice,

and I wonder what further mysteries
my body knows,
if only I were wise enough
to find them.

Four Wheels; Two Wheels;
Three

Fingers tight,
pedal, stop, pedal, stop,
pedal stop.
No speed.
Wobble back and forth from
training wheel to
training wheel,
eyes on
the ground,
terrified.

Leg over,
step onto pedals.
Push up to tall seat;
hold tightly while front man
finds center point.
Fly this tandem down a hill,
laughing behind,
trusting.

Relax back
near the ground,
hands on brakes.
Move this recumbent
anywhere.
Steering an emerging art;
free.

Addiction

Tilt-A-Whirl me to another dimension;
pin me to the back of my seat
and spin me round and round and round,
lights blurring into one long blaze,
my head back, reveling in others' screams.

Every year I waited for those moments
of captive euphoria,
brain-food for a sluggish vestibular,
pressure for a proprioceptive system
lacking the regular satisfaction of a pounding run,
a lively basketball game, a relaxing swim.

Once, slipping out of my grandparents' house,
this seven-year-old followed the siren sounds
of rumbling wheels and revving engines,
five blocks away.
My frantic parents found me grinning in the grass,
watching the battered booths sliding in different direction
and occasionally swiveling into one long spin,
found me waiting for my turn to fly.

Now, after loving the sensations of roller coasters
and water slides and Disney World,
this aging contraption seen at almost
every county fair and festival seems faded
and smaller than I remember.
But still, I stand in lines of children and harried parents
clutching my rows of tickets,
anxious to sit in my chosen booth
and grab that restraining bar.

Tilt-A-Whirl me to another dimension;
pin me to the back of my seat
and spin me round and round and round,
lights blurring into one long blaze,
my head back, reveling in others' screams.

Exposure

Perched on top of the climbing tower that summer at
Family Camp,
my harness tight, legs hanging over the lush green valley,
I wait for my feet to push my body off the wood into
that heart-in-throat whoosh down the zip line to waiting
 hands.
The kid before me is hanging at the bottom,
now released to the spongy floor,
now clambering out of the way;
The counselors signal the all-clear, shout some
 encouraging phrases,
but I can't hear past the hammering of my heart,
can't abandon my body into space despite years of
roller-coaster plunges and Ferris wheel loop-de-loops.
This isn't a passive release into programmed thrills;
this is an act of the will, a daring I haven't yet found.
The kids behind me scream, "Go!"
My mother presses my back, but my hands grip
the edge of this suddenly looming skyscraper
even as my feet become jelly.

I cannot move.
I can not move.
No movement possible.
Only rigidity, the verdant abyss below me
imploding
into blackness.
Overload.
Somehow they disconnect me, carry my body to the steps
and uncurl my legs so I can make
my mournful descent.
When will my courage come?
When, oh when will my courage come?

Confession

My favorite chairs are the kind that
seem to be squatting,
their four legs spreading out
onto soft wheels.
Usually they spin,
their backs like spines,
stretchable,
hard to resist bending until
they fall over.

I've spent too many minutes
analyzing the hums of their
rotating cores,
noting their velocity;
sometimes the seats unscrewed
and landed on the floor like
some crazy wind-machine
I'd beheaded.

Our green "Do More" chair
picked up at a garage sale

taunted me with its admonition to
"Do More"
even as I lost myself
in spinning.

We don't own any
squatting chairs now,
but I like the way our rockers
remind me of shrugging,
and the K-shape of our log chairs
on the porch,
a beloved letter.

I'm done tilting windmills.
I think I'll resign myself
to observing and
sitting.

Breathe

The little kids look like
astronauts in their clear plastic hoods
attached by hoses to an oxygen
dispenser on the wall.
The sealing ring around my neck
tickles my throat;
now I hear the whoosh
of the life-force ballooning
my own hood,
and I imagine the clear cold gas flowing
into my brain,
the pressure of this
hyperbaric chamber bringing dormant
cells to life.

Flow, oxygen, flow, bathing cells,
healing injury.

Waiting is work: over an hour of
convincing myself not to pull
this thing off my head;

my mind searches for distractions:
the Sesame Street program on the
big screen, the view out of the porthole of
this airplane-like cabin,
a magazine, my pillow.
I settle for a long stretch on the bench
as I watch the kids' feet twitch
to the music and envy their obliviousness
to sensation.
Ernie and Bert continue their patter
on the screen;
I check the clock on the outside wall every
five or ten minutes,
willing its large hand around the circle.

Nothing hurts:
I am entertained, comfortable, and warm;
I am a caged lion waiting for release;
I am a blessed man receiving nourishment.
I am all of these and more,
all together.

Flow, oxygen, flow; for sixty sessions,
bathing cells,
healing injury.

Sacrifice

They want my arm again,
those phlebotomists who spend their hours
wrapping tubing around biceps
to encourage bulging veins to rise
and spill their contents
into long clear tubes.

I watch my blood flowing freely, quickly
until the tubes are maroon with the promise
of hundreds of levels, like encrypted code,
waiting for specialists to puzzle out the state
of my organs,
the health of each vital cell.

I used to fear the needle most,
its jab like fire,
its removal, a burst of pain--
but years of B-12 shots have dulled that dread--
and after the puncture,
I used to loathe the sticky Band-Aids,

animated or plain,
and ripped their foreign substance
from my skin.

Aah, the tube's released,
my vein recedes,
new webbing's drawn round the wound.
The pathway between my intricate inside
and less impressive outside is closing,
as I leave my blood
like some precious offering
to the seers and interpreters
of life.

Borrowed Shelter

The house
creaks
like a swaying tree
as if her logs,
sawn,
stripped of bark,
milled into cylinders then
kiln-dried,
have never forgotten
their source.

Now,
her logs cross-linked from
end to end,
the house breathes
around me,
shifts,
funnels tiny bursts of
air past the chinking
laid by
careful men
two summers ago.

The house groans,
mourning its rigidity
in the midst of
the willows,
like a giant Aeolian harp
in the teeth of
the sighing wind.

Spectrum

How droll the square of blue
mixed to computer-guided specifications,
now in liquid form covering a soft roller,
transferred onto a hunter-green wall,
spreading out in all directions,
first green and blue,
then blue-green,
then its own robin's egg radiance,
obliterating the past.

Why do we choose the hues
of our environment
like clothing slipped around ourselves
for embellishment and comfort,
some of us craving grays and ivories and browns,
others a tropical paradise,
triggers of creativity and emotions
and rest?

Someday will we instantly transform our walls
at the touch of a polished button
as the science of color evolves into

the stimulation of brainwaves necessary
for a particular outcome?
Will we say,
"I'm feeling very terra-cotta this afternoon
or maybe a little Parisian green,"
or "All the lavender-lovers belong over here,
a perfect match to the pewters"?
Perhaps.

For now, I relish the messiness
of the dripping blue on my cheeks, my hair,
wiped onto my jeans like a fresh horizon
I can almost reach.

Bizarre, Bizarre

This beast hums along like it always did,
the heat-pump driven forced-air furnace
that has warmed me for the last decade,
the soothing wind that has filled my house at
thermostatically-controlled intervals.
I didn't really notice its interruption of my essays
on the latest poems introduced in class,
or my brain-packing sessions on French verbs.
Then its frequencies were simply an accompaniment
to my also-humming brain.

But now, its monstrosity fills my night hours,
all those channels snaking through my house,
sucking moisture out of my pores in exchange
for a moment's comfort.
Now its insistent entrances break open my sleep
and I find myself climbing stairs,
turning on radios,
anything to drown out its presence.

Surrounded by machines that run erratically
or constantly,
instead of birdsong, we hear air purifiers, printers,
fax machines, cell phones, televisions, even
white noise machines that muffle
all the other sounds.

So why does this whirring awaken my nerves?
And how can I transform this dragon's den
into a bower where fairies sleep?

.00001

This is the moment,
the millisecond of your existence,
the one you were destined to mark with your crossing of
 the finish line,
your perfect dismount off the balance beam,
your exquisitely-sychronized legwork in the pool,
your triple-somersault and slide into the water with your
almost-invisible splash.

This is why your parents have mortgaged their house and
lived apart or sent you away,
each day a grieving of the time they have lost, even as they
have laughed at your strength and
independence,
and wondered at your changing form.

This is the moment you have envisioned for the last decade
from the time you first heard the national anthem played
over teary-eyed people arranged
on three different levels,
and asked your mother why they were so happy about the
round circles hanging around their necks.

That was when you noticed the tears in her eyes, and
decided this must be a really important moment
and you wanted one for yourself.

This is the moment the commentators have imagined
beforehand, are analyzing now,
and will discuss with you afterwards
because it is somehow crucial for the history books, for the
progression of humanity into
greater and greater speeds, formations, unity.

The whole world is watching,
at least the billions of people near some kind of technology,
the ones who care about your sport, or those who just
happened to turn the television on,
or the ones who know your name, hometown, and what
you ate for breakfast this morning.

This moment you trip over your shoelace,
fall down on your landing,
miss an entire sequence,
announce your fallibility with a belly flop,

and the world turns away and sighs at the embarrassment of being human.

We long for better gods, wherever we can find them.

In Step

It's the Pride, the Pride of,
the Pride of the Dutchmen Marching Band
now taking their place in the
field marching competition.

"Are they ready?"
ask the announcers.
"They're always ready!" we scream.
And we are ready,
ready for the band, the band,
the band, the band, the band.

We cling to the icy bleachers;
they strut across the field,
hundreds of uniformed high-schoolers
drilled to perfection.

Their first chord resounds,
lines divide,
flags flash as dancers weave
through open ranks

to the deep staccato of the drums,
the drums, the drums,
then the brawling of the tubas and
the long trombones,
and a hush and
the sweetness of the winds,
answered by the shimmer of the brassy
brassy brass,
as the lines intersect,
then disconnect,
then find each other again,
with mincing steps forwards,
backwards, right and left,
now waves of motion spread across the field,
then a crash of cymbals,
and this vast organ of sound
draws together elegantly in
one swelling crescendo,
answered by our cheers.

Menagerie

They appear as if drawn
to my pied piper father:
a succession of pigs:
the first, strolling in front of his truck
in a nearby small town,
probably escaped from a semi;
the second, strolling in front of my sister
across our lane,
hunted down by my father and brother
and brought home for bacon;
a tame goose, strutting into our yard,
not resisting our passing her light, hollow body
from hand to hand, before strutting off again;
a woodchuck trapped in our window well,
snarling his way back to the woods;
an occasional deer risking the ire
of our tethered dogs to nibble in the garden;
two litters of wild cats in the garage,
their mothers abandoning their too-young babies
to our futile mercies.
Why are these creatures intersecting with our lives,
each leaving behind an impression, a story,

perhaps a reminder that we *homo sapiens*
never inhabit this planet
alone?

Morning
(October 20, 2011, Zanesville, Ohio)

Why did he
slink
from cage to cage
perhaps in the dark of
the early dawn
when tiger's eyes gleamed
as he slipped each latch
open?

Did he imagine their
trembling
as they stepped outside into
open space,
all the wild things,
rescued, sheltered,
now driving humans into
their shelters
until
gunfire silenced the beasts'
roaring hunger,

then silenced his hunger for
freedom from
need
as he fled the cage of
his life?

Seduction

Knife tip pressing
blood-red skin,
puncturing into
creamy flesh,
slicing down
through heart to
seeded core
then white flesh
and falling
away.
Now two parts,
flat, bare,
exposed,
lifting flesh to
tongue and teeth.
First bite.

No wonder Eve
couldn't resist
the apple.

One Hour

In the city park,
the oaks rise like long-standing sentinels
over the plastic play equipment
underlaid with wood shavings,
occasional benches scattered around.
A grizzled man glides down the path in his power chair;
two preschool boys pull themselves up the small slide,
then *bump, bump, bump* their way down the steps;
an older girl joins their play,
punctuating their prattle with her nursery songs,
while a bored woman,
sunglasses sliding down her nose,
observes their antics.
She promises her trio donuts from the nearby bakery;
one, two, three; they are gone.
A teenaged boy chugs his moped down the street,
red flag fluttering.
Now a young mother slips her infant girl into a baby swing
and eases her back and forth.
Somewhere a city utility truck reverses,
its *bee-eep, bee-eep, bee-eep* permeating the park.
Two black-haired boys swing across the overhead ladder,

slide down the tubes, then try to outdo each other on the
 swings--
pumping higher and higher--
before jumping off and clambering onto the bandshell
 stage
to practice their movie star voices.
The courthouse clock chimes once,
while a high wind sways the upper branches of the trees.

Release

When the unending staccato of voices and radios
and every other type of man-made machine
drives me outside,
I go towards the trees.

Willows—the fast-growing kind
my father and brother planted when this house
was the only obstacle on our hilltop
to the screaming winds
streaming around its shifting walls.

Now I stand beneath the arching trunks,
loving the gentle sway of their branches,
the light filtering through their leaves
enclosing me in a shimmer of gold-green,
and I walk the path that I have tramped
down one side of the row of trees and back,
my own private escape for
this pacing, pondering soul.

The house seems far away.
The ribbon of road tracing the land beyond me,

a mere decoration,
its occasional miniature cars and semis
blending into the landscape of variegated fields,
the advancing train a matter of passing interest,
a wrinkle in my view of the well-watered grounds.

Here I grasp a measure of peace
as my feet press into the clammy earth,
my thoughts rising above the wispy clouds,
floating into undared atmospheres of possibility,
my heart's rampant restlessness stilled
for a time.

Dusk

With what brushes
do you trace
this delicate outline of
branches against
flame, red, amber,
blush, purple,
colors melding into
deeper tones until
all fades into
blackness,
O artist God,
each morning choosing
a fresh palette
on one canvas of sky,
each evening displaying
another,
as if these masterpieces
revealed
at sun's rising and
setting

could never quench
your thirst for endless
possibility?

Grant me that wild joy
fresh each dawn
until I sink into
the indigo of
your new creation.

Sleep

Why do I fight
your soft embrace,
down-drifting into thoughtlessness
or fantastic dreams that seem disjunct
when surfacing through that twilight
just before I wake?

I roam the house,
quilt dragging behind me,
as if hunting for a resting place
to sink into oblivion
by a softly-playing radio
or a heat duct, or even
my bed.

Perhaps my solitude seems most stark
without a warm partner
in this descent,
canine or human to breathe beside,
drape an arm over,
find in the deep darkness.

Fuzzy-headed, my body craves hours
in your company
while my mind fights for
one more minute
alone.

Attempt

Try talking when your mouth doesn't say
what your mind intends,
no matter how persistent its commands;
try talking when your words repeat incessantly
whether you want them to or not.

Try talking when your mouth acts like it's filled with
    marbles
so your phrases sound garbled and childish;
try talking when you speak much louder
than you should, as if your volume controls
are stuck on high.

Try talking when the results of most efforts
make you want to cry instead
but you can't stop jabbering because
your brain is stuck on automatic.

Try listening to the television announcers carrying on
their endless commentary,
and to the professors releasing their

nuggets of wisdom,
and to your classmates teasing each other,
and knowing that you have the perfect comeback
but no one may ever hear you say it.

Just try. Just try. And try again.

Resolution

I have done it all,
years of therapy and supplements
and detoxification.
Every new hope on my dismal
horizon, I have embraced,
for hope is a giddy thing.

I have conquered class after class,
finally carrying
that coveted diploma,
but still, when the waiter takes
my order in a restaurant,
he thinks I cannot
comprehend him.

Must I carry my A papers in
Western Civilization
everywhere I go?

The inside is not the outside.
The outside is not the inside.

I will not shrink.

I will never relent.

I will never stop reaching you.

So You Know

For those who assume I cannot
speak English clearly enough
to be understood,
know this:
I am a student of languages,
a dabbler in Arabic phrases, with
a semester of Spanish and
a year of French
behind me.

My "Ola" and "Parlez-vous francais?"
may lack your crisp
enunciation of
syllables, but
I will master Sanskrit
and Italian
if I please,
so how will you answer
that?

Reaching

On our way through customs,
English disappears,
replaced by rivers of syllables
that little resemble the Spanish
of my college summer.
The official manages a few English phrases
before waving us by,
then reverts back to another volley
of unintelligible sounds.
Animated conversations flourish around us,
the speakers' faces and gestures
insufficient clues to their subjects.

Two young American boys chatter
all the way to our hotel,
sliding between languages like trapeze artists
swinging between podiums,
translating our needs
to the nodding, smiling driver.

At the reception desk, we relax
as the clerk answers my father's questions

in accented English.
Elsewhere, I watch my mother play
my association game,
pairing single words with exaggerated pointing,
frustrated by shaking heads and kind smiles.
Ah, this is my life, my life.
But I understand it all, yet look as foolish as you,
as elementary in my expression.
Now we struggle together, all of us in this new place
where sound and meaning flow in uncertain connections,
bound by our need to be known.

Disconnected

Hunched over,
burdened by my tortoise-shell of
books,
I see you fly past me,
hare on wheels,
hero of a modern fable.

Whoever thinks plodding is
the only way to win
this race,
never met this
generation,
riders of innovation,
of light beams into Trekkian futures.

I'm the only one who takes
ten years to
get through college--
two classes a semester,
my mind racing while my body
plods along.

Will someone discover how
to help this tortoise fly
with you?

Risk

All I needed was a set of earphones
and my favorite Raffi tapes back then,
to begin the day in one city
and sleep in another,
never minding the machinations of
that giant silver bird,
its vibrations pulsing through my feet,
adding to the rhythms of the
Beluga whale.
Take-offs were exhilarating,
the rising shriek of the engines
part of my library of
Really Cool Sounds,
sounds I would later replicate on
my Casio keyboard.
Flying was a negotiable passage.

Until 9/11.

Everyone asks the "Where were you?" question.
I was early for Theology 101,
watching the planes hitting the buildings

as my classmates trickled in.
One month later, we flew to Disney World
and suddenly that plane was
a potential weapon,
one that I longed to escape almost
as soon as we left the ground.

They tell me I'm far more likely to die in
the inferno of a car crash than
that airborne collision burned into
my memory, and they sing to me
as the wheels touch down
and we wait for the signal to deplane,
lest I force my way through the crowd
even before the door is open.

We are none of us the same anymore.

Lost Friend (II)

She drags herself from
the porch to
the circle of
our gathered family,
her amber eyes dull
with pain
for one last caress before
dying.

Grown now,
we still flinch at
our mother's words,
"We have to do this,"
as we stroke this childhood
comrade and watch
our father gather
the glass bottle,
tube,
and needle
from his truck.

For fourteen years, Elsie began
each walk by
jumping up and barking, then
turning and dashing away
down gravel roads and into
water-logged ditches, then
clearing fences and sprinting across
seemingly endless fields,
an amber streak of joy,
finally following us home,
panting.

Last week, she stood
at the end of the driveway,
the growth in her body
inoperable,
her tail still wagging
slightly,
eyes blank.

Now, we shiver as
my father performs
the unwanted work of
his profession,

this time for all of us.
but mostly,
for her,
his quiet, patient hands
inserting, adjusting,
waiting.

"She'll just go to sleep," he says,
and she is drifting away,
but before her body stills,
she howls,
perhaps the medicine reaching
her heart
or her farewell
to us.

We bury her under
the willows
and
weep.

Midsummer Night

Zipped up from feet to neck,
I lie engulfed in this womb-like tent
just large enough for me to stretch out,
walls touching hair and feet,
each move a slide against the nylon,
night sounds a thin partition away.
All is damp from the momentary shower
filtering through pine trees overhead,
trickling into unsealed corners.
Nearby zippers whoosh up and down
as fellow campers collect necessities before
they too enclose themselves
in our transient community of domes,
like giant mushrooms sheltering wood sprites
soon slipping into the odiferous slumbers
of the deep woods,
the crickets chirruping our lullabies,
the creaking woods, our cradle.

Unbound

Oh the Hills, the Black Hills,
dark with trees, mystery,
Paha Sapa in Lakota,
sacred Sioux sanctuary.
You have worked your magic on us,
clambering up rocks like
yesterday's children,
egging each other on
to greater heights,
each one more breath-filling than
the next.

We were wild young things playing on
God's obstacle course,
even those with graying hair
suddenly goat-footed, deep-chested,
awed and awesome in strength
as if released from straitjackets
of occupation and debt.

We scoured your gold mines,
roamed through your herds of wild buffalo,

fed your burros,
swam your icy lakes,
stumbled through your Badlands-
God-painted pottery--
listened to your wolves,
surprised your deer,
smelled your fires,
shivered in your morning mists,
left you with regret.

The Fabulous Four Minus Three

The house feels gaping
without them
even if they only came
home from school
to lie on the couches doing
their homework or
to practice their contest pieces down
in the basement where
they wouldn't be
so loud.
A trombone and saxophone could
be blaring, but
my sister's flute just made me
want to sleep,
her notes like spun sugar.

I didn't know I'd miss
their catfights,
all drama and making up,
and their friends dropping by
whenever,

and the cookies they made
when they needed comfort.

Six people around the table
somehow seems more jolly than three,
especially when we're all adults now,
not adults-in-the-making.

They call us from
other states and apartments,
their voices on speaker phone inserted
into the atmosphere,
but I want their jackets hanging
over the rocking chair,
their perfumes and after-shave drifting
past me,
their addresses the same
as mine.

(In)dependence

Maybe the Asians have the right idea.
Or the Africans.
These communal societies where
the "I" is really a "We"
and the welfare of all matters more
than the transcendence of one.
We loners are constantly playing
this porcupine game:
repelling our potential competitors,
lovers, controllers,
then huddling together for warmth
but never close enough
for the comforting balm of connection
to saturate our desperate hearts.
Why do we hope that large houses and cars
will fill our empty spaces,
that business relationships will move beyond
the last sale,
that casual liasons will plant anything
but sickness and the craving for even deeper
intimacy?

Look at the Godhead: Father, Son, and Holy Spirit.
One in Three and Three in One.
Designed in His/Her/Their image,
could we crave anything else but uniqueness
in the heart of
unity?

Emma

Four Char-peis and a Shepherd feasted
on fallen deer
on the grassy meridian.

Puppy mill fodder, we thought.

On Easter morning, they fled our
rescue mission, all save one which
we trapped in a culvert and
brought home, where she huddled
in our laundry room,
impassive.

We stroked her big wrinkle
of a face;
she flinched, her eyes cold,
wary.

What tall, deep-voiced man
terrorized this gentle spirit?

For months, she held herself
at the outer range of
our reach,
her tail wagging.

Thankfully, she risked love,
belly up.

Now we lay by our fire together,
at peace.

Rest
for Sarah

You see me--
spirit nodding to spirit,
my body's gyrations irrelevant
to our continuing
dialogue,
the tapping keyboard
merely a conduit
from mind to heart.

Friend.

You surround me
with uncommon recognition
and my submerged self blinks
at this sudden light,
breathes in this essential atmosphere
so often denied me,
in great gasps,
like a drowning man
raised to the welcoming sun.

When you drive away,
I watch you from my window,
calculate the days, hours, minutes, seconds
before our next encounter
when we will savor
the satisfaction
of seeing each other
again.

Passage

We are changing lanes, searching for our exit,
maneuvering past the merging traffic, just beyond a
   belching truck
when the big-bellied plane flashes over the overpass,
skimming above the electric lines
on its way to the Minneapolis airport.

From my sister's apartment window,
white knuckled, I watch the jets heading for the runway,
seeming to barely miss the trees in their rapid descent,
relentless in their mission to touch down and release their
temporary community
to their next appointments on time.

All day and through the inky darkness, I hear the planes
   come in
and think of other sleepers in other houses hearing
them roar into the clouds;
in airports around the earth this incessant pattern weaving
travelers in and out to unlimited destinations;
while I crunch my morning toast, this living web of
movement and light carries

the people of this globe to fresh experiences, connections
destinies,
each ascent a farewell to something or someone,
each descent, a greeting.

Grounded, I long for the savannas of Africa,
the hang-gliders of Hawaii,
the mosaics of the Middle East,
the castles of Europe--
these riches only released to those brave enough
to trust their bodies to hours of confined suspension
miles above *terra firma*,
diverted by movies playing on their iPads,
untroubled by their seatmate's breath.

Soon, soon men will stamp my passport
and I will pit my hunger for adventure against
my craving for groundedness and solitude,
second by second,
as I weave through the troposphere
in search of my next hello.

Flight

I like to think of interesting ways to transcend
the limitations of my life,
like the square-faced man in "Up" who raises his tiny
    cottage with balloons,
or Frodo in "Lord of the Rings" stepping outside his door,
or the hardest scene yet, the men pushing through the
    underground tunnel
in "The Great Escape."
We are always pushing boundaries, it seems.
Such is the germ of living,
the cocoon into butterfly story.
Movies are a short-term fix, the borrowing of others'
    imagination;
travel magazines start me wondering about the lives I
    might have lived elsewhere;
vacations are a breather from the tedium of normalcy,
but prayer is best of all, an intrusion into a heaven beyond
    heavens,
this tiny speck of a man touching a Being so big
that even Michelangelo's glorious scene on the Sistine
    Chapel ceiling
cannot begin to encompass the impossibility

of that reach into eternity.
But I like to live there for awhile each day
outside of time and all the discouragements of this planet
Then I come back, reluctantly,
glad for another breath, a hug,
a sip of mocha,
a sleep festooned with dreams.

Unexpected

Not to be bought for any price,

this Love falling into my hard heart

so nothing I might do prevents its coming,

this Love falling into my hard heart

and crashing through blockades of just crazy fear,

this Love falling into my hard heart

swirling around them until they come right down

this Love falling into my hard heart

into the recesses of swollen pain

his Love falling into my hard heart

like sweet balm pouring into bloody wounds

this Love falling into my hard heart

and relief saturating new-healed skin,

this Love falling into my hard heart

softening the calluses, defenses against hurt,

this Love falling into my hard heart

clearing away deadness, leaving vibrant strength,

this Love falling into my hard heart

this Love powering my young heart.

Grace

This time, like royals attending
a coronation, the professors marched in
resplendent robes, while the organ,
its silver pipes climbing to the ceiling,
thundered out a blessing to the
families waiting for their scholar
to receive his or her due reward,
all holding one collective breath,
their video cameras whirring and
flashbulbs popping like confetti
on an already-glittering scene.

I was just praying that I wouldn't trip
on the way down the aisle,
wouldn't rip off the irksome robe,
or the crazy hat, its tassel tickling
my face, rip it off with the loud "hutz!"
that used to explode from me when
my body had tolerated its limit,
wouldn't forget which hand to extend
to receive the college president's
congratulations,

wouldn't drop the diploma on the way
back to my seat.

The list of graduates seemed interminable;
my mother and I quietly counting backwards
from 100, sometimes by 3's and 5's,
whatever distracted this mind from
its pressing anxieties,
familiar tool in so many classes when discipline
gave way to silliness, now critical for this moment
that I couldn't, wouldn't desecrate with
my behaviors.

Marlys gave me a nudge; I stood.
We walked a little together,
then I stepped forward alone,
and took the diploma,
shook the warm hand,
and turned back to a wave of forbidden applause
spreading like rain, glorious rain,
all over this trembling form.

Perchance

Boy meets girl--
the oldest story on earth.
Girl decides:
she turns to boy and stays;
she lingers for awhile, then leaves;
she walks away.
Everything depends upon
that first look,
that first whiff of pheromones,
that first handshake,
that first smile
or grimace.
Everything.

Eastern Star

What can I offer you, fair dove,
I have not given before,
while you, eyes glowing with fresh love
seek yet to give me more?

Your flowing hair, a stream of silk;
your lips, a taste of mead;
your shoulders white as camel's milk;
your heart, a fiery steed.

We ride enlightened through black nights
by heaven's blaze of stars,
then sample earth's most rich delights
and dream of ancient czars

by desert palms and limpid pools,
refreshed, till day is through.
Ah love, I'll drape your neck with jewels
and blaze the world with you!

Just Go

Oh little sister,

gliding between white rows

of chairs

under a willow,

the lake-breeze lifting your satin gown

in time to the falling

notes of the harp

and classical guitar,

he is waiting for you,

his smile like the warm

invitation of this July

evening,

beneath a canopy of

ribbons.

Couples

I watch the way their eyes mesh,
their expressions like mirrors reflecting the other's
irritation, bliss, boredom, contentment,
hunger,
their lacing fingers sending rivulets of grace
from one hand to the other,
their voices low,
their bodies drawn towards each other
as if dwelling in their own invisible retreat
oblivious to the observers
around them.

We who feign interest
in the closest magazine or newspaper
cannot deny the spirit flowing between them,
covet their sure fit,
like electrified Legos,
or mortals under some Midsummer's Eve spell.

Others bear the long-worn emblems of loyalty
on their left hands,

but their gazes are disjunct,
their conversational attempts clashing,
their eyes ringed with sorrow,
their shoulders stiff with impatience
at the length of each other's sentences,
their bodies separating to inhabit other spaces
as if desperate for some measure of peace.

And I wonder if this ardent pair will slip
into indifference
when the days, weeks, months, and years
of survival bring dreams down into delusions,
novelty into monotony,
hope into bleakness,
or will this current flow untroubled
like a river through the rocky canyons of their life
cutting a pathway wildly, uniquely their own?

Lightkeepers

Tuxedoed and barefoot in the cool April sand,
my baby brother, all six feet, four inches of his sheltering
    frame,
reaches for his dark-haired bride,
holding her gaze like some treasure unearthed in this
    afternoon light.

Later, mid pink punch and spring-green cupcakes,
I listen to my Honorary Best Man's speech
issuing from the other Best Man's lips,
glad that this gathering of significant friends
smile at the right places, as they hear my message
to this new creation, two now one.

I offer the usual greetings, thanks, memories
and blessings to the crowd,
but I want to tell this love-struck couple:
"*Look* at each other,
Look at the eternal spirit-being whose life
is now bonded with yours,
clothed in temporary finery, but possessing
his or her own beauty and dignity."

"Never let the crassness of daily commerce
dull your respect for each other's glory,
reflected light from Him who is All Light.
Protect, cherish, and encourage each other's divine spark
no matter how different from your own,
for you have specific tasks to complete,
separately and together,
before you enter the next glistening kingdom."

But I am not Gandalf the Grey
and this is not some fantasy
with brave hobbits and beautiful elves
and evil dragons to vanquish.

Still, I wonder if anyone thinks of destinies anymore
or the shortness of the time
we are given,
and I step outside into the twilight
bearing a little of the radiance of this day
into the coming darkness.

On the Airwaves

Instantly,
we surrender to
the melody filtering through
our brain circuits,
opening the story
we now inhabit
through the vibrations of her spirit-voice
calling into our routine,
"I am here.
Do you hear me?"
Without her intrusion
would we ever stop
to notice?

Longing

In the middle of my Starbuck's caramel macchiato,
heaven invades,
its messengers proclaimed over the mall sound system,
skies bedecked with angels,
glistening,
their *glorias* curling from golden mouths
over grubby shepherds crouching on dusty hills,
wishing for a little sleep, for heaven's sake;
just a warm meal and a heavy cloak and a soft cleft of
    earth,
not this celestial extravaganza,
a vision too rich for staring eyes,
too much for hammering hearts.
And all for what?
To find a newborn in a grimy shed,
his young parents assaulted by the smells,
just longing for peace after a trying day,
not the interruption of these babbling men
gesticulating into the air,
telling wild tales of shining beings leading them
to this place.

Did Mary and Joseph smile knowingly
at the bafflement of these men of the plains,
remember their own confusion
when the veil between realms parted
and they, too, faced the radiant ones,
all for this child resting at their feet?

Inconvenient, the disruption of our
focused lives,
the appearance of a supernatural Being
requiring all—
the surrender of raised hands,
the worship of reluctant hearts.
Will I put my coffee down,
even for a moment,
and add my assent to the angels' anthems,
or will I ignore this summons to a higher realm,
to the eternal celebration?

Ah look,
my heart ascends beyond
my grasping will
to its natural resting place
before the Throne.

Coming Down

They say the Glory is coming this year
like the cloud that led Israel through the desert.
Swirls of that cloud are appearing in churches,
in homes, over a friend's head.

Do you believe in heavenly fireworks,
in galaxies beyond galaxies,
in a Presence that reveals itself
in snowstorms and quasars?
Why not clouds of gold and smoke?

I like to imagine that cloud filling my room
surrounded by muscular angels
with shimmering swords,
me prostrate,
while every cell returns to its
original design.

I am weeping with relief, with joy
that, at last, everything
has been made
new.

Move

Why such yearning
to stretch out the leg,
to bend the spine into a graceful arc,
arms tracing the sky,
to leap,
to land on bent knees,
to beat the hands on the floor,
on the thighs,
to kick and stomp and clap,
to roll,
then reach up tall, undulating,
like a white birch
in the cold wind,
to spin,
eyes gazing at one fixed point,
head whipping round at the
last possible second,
to shimmy the shoulders,
the hips, the feet,
to flutter the fingers,
to mark the pulse

of the pivoting world,
to kiss the Creator,
to dance?

Rumination

Writing in Barnes and Noble
is like forcing my way through a crowd of ideas,
my words falling beneath
the thousands of volumes exhaling
life stories, viewpoints, newest methods, maudlin tales,
even horror into the atmosphere,
accompanied by Sinatra's crooning to full orchestra.

We are, all of us, trying to get
Somewhere, to gain Someone's
attention, to sell
Something.

Why push?
Why struggle through the international
thesaurus of meanings and inferences
to select and arrange those that
convey the need, want, hope of
one spirit to another,
why convince, enlighten, perhaps
even navigate the heart?

Porquoi?

The discount table mocks my ambition;
six-ninety-nine for two years of a
writer's life,
now on clearance,
maybe out of print,
soon forgotten for the next
new name, new vision for
this wobbling earth.

Still,
as I seek the comfort of
other traveler's scribblings,
I will not deny them
mine.

Awakenings

Sometimes they come to us like faint images bursting
with the lushness of Renaissance paintings;
there and gone,
yet lovely enough to force our heads onto our palms
in the effort of grasping a silken thread
to reel the voluptuous beauties back into our sight--
perhaps a little threadbare this time,
and missing their gilt decorations,
but brilliant, nevertheless;
worthy of incarnating on this shabbier earth.

Sometimes they seem the most plodding of mantras,
the soundtracks of stultifying dreams that we wish
we could escape,
our only release their recording on paper or screen
so that they will let us alone.
Days later, our entries appear transfigured,
enchanting, maybe even a little wise,
perchance, vital messages from the unknown.

Sometimes they are fireflies flitting around
the peripheries of our consciousness,

maddening,
their hypnotic lights blinking,
difficult to grasp for more than a second
before they disappear,
or, even worse, lie dead,
their possibilities extinguished,
their glitter gone.

Sometimes they begin as rough sketches
scratched into the clay,
like designs for a Gothic cathedral,
diminished and expanded through endless revision,
pondered in the mind's eye
for year beyond year
as each chiseled thought is set in place,
finally rising into resplendent symmetry,
glowing with the beauty of Light
far beyond our imaginings,
a sanctuary for aching souls.

Rarely, they arrive like precious manuscripts
ready for binding,
their polished forms spilling perfectly
onto the page,

lacking only their author's remarks
and tooled leather covers
before finding their honored place
on ancient shelves,
joining the voices of centuries past.

Then we pause, and wonder at this bounty
trusted to our wavering minds,
wonder at the ways we receive
these fragments of truth to assemble
and disperse into the restless universe,
wonder why we watch and listen
and will not let them go.

About the Author

As a child, Craig Romkema's access to the world was limited by sensory and communication difficulties. When he discovered supported typing around the age of ten, he was able to, as he wrote one day, "finally let someone know whether I wanted a peanut butter or a jelly sandwich, because my mouth would always say 'jelly'!" Craig transitioned from an alphabet board to a computer, and quickly moved into regular classrooms where he was able to share the thoughts he had been pondering for so many years alone.

Following high school graduation, Craig completed his first book of poetry, *Embracing The Sky* (Jessica Kingsley Publishers, 2002). He then spent his next decade composing college essays, and in 2011, earned his degree in English Literature from Dordt College in Sioux Center, Iowa.

You can follow Craig's blog at craigromkema.wordpress.com.